Dress Rehearsal

A Play

Alec Baron

Samuel French – London
New York – Sydney – Toronto – Hollywood

FOR AMATEUR PRODUCTION ENQUIRIES

UNITED KINGDOM AND WORLD
EXCLUDING NORTH AMERICA
plays@samuelfrench.co.uk
020 7255 4302/01

Each title is subject to availability from Samuel French, depending upon country of performance.

CHARACTERS

Mrs Flutterstone, (playing **Britannia**)
Mrs Grandway, the producer
Mrs Hamberley, the wardrobe mistress
Mrs Pinkerton, the assistant wardrobe mistress
Miss Warburton, (playing **Queen Elizabeth**)
Miss Pomerance, the authoress
Mrs Burncliffe, (playing **Queen Victoria**)
Mr Trotter, the stage manager
Mr Thirlstane, (playing **Henry VIII**)

Time—the present

Other plays by Alec Baron
published by Samuel French

The Big Cats
Chimera
Company Come

DRESS REHEARSAL

An empty stage. A dress rehearsal by an amateur dramatic group of a costume show is in progress

When the Curtain *rises Mrs Flutterstone, dressed as Britannia, is sitting, as on an old penny, holding her shield and spear. There is a Union Jack behind her. She sits quite still for about twenty seconds, then looks out front; she has difficulty shielding her eyes from the Lights because both her hands are full*

Mrs Flutterstone (*shouting into the audience*) How much longer do you want me to sit here like a waxwork at a wake?

Mrs Grandway, the producer, who is out front in the audience, comes on to the stage

Mrs Grandway Now now, Mrs Flutterstone, please have a little patience. (*She calls*) I think that will do, Mrs Hamberley, don't you?

Mrs Hamberley, the wardrobe mistress, appears from the wings. She is an overdressed, overbearing lady, the kind that takes on all the top jobs and does very little. She is followed by Mrs Pinkerton, the assistant wardrobe mistress, rather timid but efficient; she is overburdened with work but continually apologetic, and over-powered by Mrs Hamberley

What do you think, Mr Trotter?

Mr Trotter, the stage manager, bounces on from the other side of the stage, a buoyant little man

They all contemplate Britannia

Mrs Hamberley There's something wrong with the helmet—I don't know what—but there is.

Mrs Pinkerton It isn't the helmet, Mrs Hamberley. I think it might be the shoes.

Mrs Hamberley Oh, the shoes as well. You're quite right, Mrs Pinkerton. She'd never have shoes like that. Not to rule the waves in!

Mr Trotter Would you like a bit more light on that helmet, Mrs Grandway? We could hit her head with that spare spot on the number two batten.

Mrs Flutterstone You mind what you're doing, Mr Trotter.

Mr Trotter (*ignoring her*) I could put a fifty-two Gold in it. Make it shine a treat that would. Like a new penny!

Mrs Hamberley (*to Mrs Grandway*) If you light that helmet more, Mrs Grandway, it will just show up what's wrong with it more. Because it's not right, you know.

Mrs Grandway The helmet looks all right from the front, Mrs Hamberley. Yes, Mr Trotter, can you do that? A fifty-two Gold would be splendid.

Mr Trotter I'll have to get the steps then.

Mr Trotter exits

Mrs Hamberley I still think it's the wrong helmet, you know.

Mrs Pinkerton (*apologetically*) It came with the costume. They should know.

Mrs Hamberley You can't rely on them, unfortunately. They often send the wrong thing if they haven't got the one you want, or the size you want. You weren't with us when we did that Greek play—the costumes they sent weren't Greek at all! They were Roman! And *we* didn't know, of course. Not till the headmaster of St Bartholomew's told us. We felt such fools!

Mrs Pinkerton Well *that* costume looks British enough.

Mrs Hamberley How do you mean, British? *I've* never seen anyone wearing anything like that in this country!

Mrs Flutterstone You have now!

Mrs Pinkerton I mean . . . Britannia wouldn't wear anything that wasn't British, would she?

Mrs Flutterstone Well the spear's African, isn't it? It's what the Zulus carry. And this shield says "Made in Taiwan". Look!

Mrs Hamberley Have *you* ever seen anyone in Britain wearing anything like that, Mrs Grandway?

Mrs Pinkerton It's *ancient* Britain, Mrs Hamberley, that's why.

Mrs Hamberley (*not to be beaten*) *Ancient* Britain? With a Union Jack? The Union Jack only came in when we conquered India, didn't it, Mrs Grandway? Can't be all that ancient!

Mrs Grandway It came in after the Wars of the Roses I believe, Mrs Hamberley, but I think the costume is basically Roman.

Mrs Hamberley Looks more Greek than the Roman ones we had for the Greek play. We'll have to be careful, you know, he's coming on Tuesday, the headmaster of St Bartholomew's. We wouldn't want . . . (*She stops, as an idea strikes her*) I know—has anybody got an old penny?

Nobody has

Mrs Flutterstone Must be a lot warmer in Greece than it is in here, I'm fair frozen. Do you think we could push on?

Mr Trotter comes on with the steps, erects them immediately in front of Britannia, and climbs up. Half-way up he stops

Mr Trotter (*to Britannia*) Do you think you could hold these steps for me, Mrs Flutterstone? I don't feel steady unless someone's holding them. Not since I fell off. I didn't enjoy that one bit!
Mrs Grandway *Careless Rapture.*
Mr Trotter Eh?
Mrs Grandway That's when you fell off. When we were doing *Careless Rapture.*
Mr Trotter Oh, I thought you said "Careless Rupture".
Mrs Grandway *Could* you hold his ladder, Mrs Flutterstone, please?
Mrs Flutterstone How the William Tell can I? I'm holding this spear and shield, aren't I.
Mr Trotter Well put them down a minute.
Mrs Flutterstone I'm not disturbing my dress! Mrs Pinkerton spent goodness knows how long arranging it! (*She indicates Mrs Hamberley*) Why can't *she* do it?
Mrs Hamberley Now don't exaggerate. Ten minutes it took her, no more. I was standing watching. (*Magnanimously*) I'll hold your ladder, Mr Trotter!

Mrs Hamberley holds the ladder and Mr Trotter climbs up

Miss Warburton, dressed as Queen Elizabeth I, peeps in from the wings, creeps on rather sheepishly, and whispers something to Mrs Hamberley

Mrs Hamberley (*letting go the ladder and coming to the front to speak to Mrs Grandway*) Queen Elizabeth would like a word with you, Mrs Grandway.

Mrs Grandway Not just now, Miss Warburton—we're dealing with Britannia. Can it wait? We'll call you.

Miss Warburton All right. But it's a bit draughty sitting in that dressing-room. The radiator's gone off again.

Mrs Grandway Ask Sir Walter Raleigh if he'll lend you his cloak. It looked a nice warm one to me. Fur lined.

Miss Warburton Yes, all right. Thank you.

Miss Warburton wanders off, rather aimlessly

Mrs Hamberley That woman walks about like a blindfolded man looking for a door in the wrong wall!

Mr Trotter (*shouting*) Albert! (*Then*) Hey, who's holding this ladder?!

Mrs Hamberley Oh, sorry. (*She holds it again*)

Mr Trotter (*shouting*) Switch it on, Albert.

Everyone looks up. Nothing happens

(*He calls again*) Number fourteen I think it is.

Everyone stands as if waiting for the eclipse but no light goes on

Is your dimmer down, Albert?

Nothing happens

Must be a fuse then. Check the fuse.

All the Lights go out

Not the main fuse, you nit!

The Lights come up again

(*He comes down, closes the step-ladder, catching Britannia's dress, and starts to go off, dragging her by the skirt*) I'm sorry, Mrs Grandway. It's probably the bulb. I'll get a spare tomorrow.

Mrs Flutterstone (*screaming*) Hey, I'm caught!

Mr Trotter (*stopping*) I do wish you'd be a bit more careful, Mrs Flutterstone, you could have had me over! (*He releases her skirt*)

Mr Trotter exits

Mrs Hamberley That was sheer carelessness, Mrs Flutterstone! We'd have had to pay for that costume if it would have torn!

Mrs Flutterstone But that wasn't *my* ...

Mrs Pinkerton is fussing around rearranging Britannia's skirt

Mrs Grandway Thank you, Mrs Pinkerton. The trouble is, I think, Britannia doesn't look right sitting like that.

Mrs Flutterstone How do you want me to sit? I'm sitting like Britannia sits—on me bottom!

Mrs Grandway No, I didn't mean you, Mrs Flutterstone, I meant that Britannia ought to be on a higher level than the others—symbolic—elevated—up in the air.

Mrs Flutterstone I can't stand heights, Mrs Grandway. I'd better tell you now. I go dizzy. I'd fall off.

Mrs Grandway I wasn't suggesting the top of Blackpool Tower, Mrs Flutterstone, just a small rostrum. (*She calls*) Mr Trotter!

All the ladies call "Mr Trotter"

Mr Trotter enters

Mrs Grandway Do we have a rostrum that we could put Britannia on?

Mr Trotter A rostrum? How big?

Mrs Grandway Oh, about . . . you know, just big enough for her to sit on.

Mr Trotter exits

Miss Pomerance, the authoress, strides on. A forceful, rather masculine lady, but wearing bright-coloured clothes

Miss Pomerance Mrs Grandway, if my play is ever to go on, you'll have to move faster than this. Can we get on with it? We'll have to be out of here before we know it and I haven't heard a single one of my words yet. You *did* tell me to be here for five-thirty, didn't you?

Mrs Grandway I am sorry, Miss Pomerance, but we have to get the technicalities right, you know. That's what Dress Rehearsals are for.

Miss Pomerance But this is a *play*, Mrs Grandway, not just a—a costume parade—or a historical tableau. People *say* things, they have *dialogue*.

Mrs Grandway The costumes, and the lighting of them, are very important in the kind of play you have written for us, Miss Pomerance. It's almost a—a pageant, you know.

Miss Pomerance I do know, and I'm very grateful to you for your attention to detail, but I think the words are important too. I wouldn't have written them if I didn't think so. What people say is infinitely more important than what they wear.

Mrs Grandway Ah—that's where we part company, Miss Pomerance. I know you've had a half-hour play on the radio, but this is *theatre* you know, not radio. It's the advantage we have over radio and we must exploit it. I do wish you'd leave it to me and let me get on with it.

Miss Pomerance (*after a couple of venomous beats*) Very well!!

Miss Pomerance strides off

Miss Pinkerton has now arranged the folds of Britannia's dress to Mrs Hamberley's apparent satisfaction

Mrs Hamberley How's that, Mrs Grandway?

Mrs Grandway Oh, that's excellent, Mrs Hamberley. Thank you. I hope it looks as well on the night. You won't have much time to arrange it in, you know.

Mr Trotter backs on with a rostrum, folded, the other end held by Mr Thirlstane, dressed as William Shakespeare

Mr Trotter I've found a rostrum, Mrs Grandway.

Mrs Grandway Who are *you* supposed to be, Mr Thirlstane?

Mr Thirlstane (*a meek man*) Henry the Eighth.

Mrs Grandway I thought so. But that's the William Shakespeare costume you've got on!

Mr Thirlstane I know.

Mrs Grandway You know?

Mr Thirlstane I was going to ask you about that. Would it matter all that much?

Mrs Grandway Good lord!! Of *course* it matters!

Mr Thirlstane They're both the same period, nearly, aren't they?

Mrs Grandway No, they're not! And besides, that's irrelevant, Mr Thirlstane!

Mr Thirlstane Well the Henry the Eighth costume is much too big. I look daft in it.

Mrs Flutterstone You don't look all that bright in *that* one!

Mr Thirlstane resents that and looks hurt, but says nothing

Mrs Hamberley It's supposed to be big. There should be some padding come with that Henry the Eighth costume. Have you looked for the padding?

Mrs Pinkerton I asked for the padding when I wrote. I sent Mr Thirlstane's measures.

Mr Thirlstane The trouble is that William Shakespeare—I mean Mr Huskisson—can't get into this costume. It's *much* too small for him. The Henry the Eighth costume fits him beautifully.

Mrs Hamberley (*to Mrs Pinkerton*) You must have got their measures mixed up! You've landed us in a fine pickle now, haven't you!

Mrs Pinkerton No, I didn't, honestly, I can show you the copy.

Mrs Grandway *Would* you go along to the men's dressing-room, Mrs Hamberley, and sort this out. You'll probably find some inlay in the Shakespeare costume to let out. There usually is.

Mrs Hamberley Yes, of course. You'd better come with, Mrs Pinkerton. I may be the wardrobe mistress, but if there's any sewing to do—I'm just hopeless. I've *never* had to do any, you see!

Mrs Hamberley, Mr Thirlstane and Mrs Pinkerton exit

Mr Trotter Where do you want this, Mrs Grandway?

Mrs Grandway There at the back. In the centre.

Mr Trotter Where she's sitting now?

Mrs Grandway Yes, but a shade further back, I think—we don't want the rostrum to interfere with the ensemble grouping later.

Mr Trotter If we take it farther back we'll have to do the Britannia lighting again.

Mrs Grandway It'll have to be done again, anyhow—she'll be higher up.

Mr Trotter True. I forgot about that. OK Britannia, let's be having you. Right, Mr Thirlstane, grab hold. (*He looks around*) Where's he gone?

Mrs Grandway He's gone to get his costume sorted out.

Mr Trotter I can't manage this on my own.

Miss Pomerance enters

Miss Pomerance I'll help you Mr Trotter, or we'll never get started. No point in hanging around all night doing nothing!

As they erect the rostrum in place Britannia comes down front carrying her spear and shield

Mrs Flutterstone Do you think I could go and get a drink out of my flask of coffee, Mrs Grandway? It's in the dressing-room.

Mrs Grandway Not just now, Mrs Flutterstone. Just wait until we get your position settled.

Mrs Flutterstone I'm fair starved to the marrow in this. If they don't get the heating sorted out for tomorrow Miss Pomerance won't be able to hear her precious words for me teeth chattering and me knees knocking.

Mrs Grandway I'll speak to someone about it in the morning.

Miss Warburton timidly enters

Miss Warburton Have you a minute *now*, Mrs Grandway?

Mrs Grandway Yes, all right Miss Warburton, let me have a look at you.

Miss Warburton strikes a queenly pose

Walk up and down.

She does so, the queenliness alas gone

Ye—s . . . the costume is splendid, Miss Warburton—but could you walk a little more like a queen?

Miss Warburton gives little waves of acknowledgement left and right

No, I mean more *erect*. Stand up straight. Hold your bottom in. Hold your head high. Chin up. Higher.

Miss Warburton follows all instructions. She walks with her chin up so high that were not Mrs Grandway to shout a warning she would fall over Miss Pomerance who is bending down to help pick up the rostrum top

Not so high that you can't see where you're going. Yes, I think we'll get away with that. I suppose that's as queenly as you can manage.

Miss Warburton I'll practise in the bedroom tonight, Mrs Gradway.

Mrs Flutterstone (*feeling the material of Queen Elizabeth's dress*) It's a lot warmer than this stuff. I'd have played Queen Elizabeth if I'd have known she was going to have something warm to wear. It was offered to me first, Queen Elizabeth was.

Miss Warburton Oh, I wish you would have done.

Mrs Grandway Queen Elizabeth was a little flatter-chested than you are, Miss Warburton, judging by the portraits. Do you think you could do something about that?

Miss Warburton I'll see what I can fix up ... in the bedroom tonight.

Mrs Grandway Did you get another chance to look at your lines?

Miss Warburton I look at them all the time, Mrs Grandway, honestly I do. (*A hunted look comes on to her face*) I get them off pat, and the minute I come on to the stage my mind goes a blank. I hardly slept last night for worrying.

Mrs Grandway We're all relying on you. We don't want any prompts, do we? Miss Pomerance won't like it if you forget her lines, will she?

Miss Warburton (*with a fearful glance towards Miss Pomerance*) No. I'll look at them again, tonight. In the ...

Mrs Flutterstone It's going to be busy in your bedroom tonight for a change, isn't it?

Miss Warburton (*after a harsh look at Mrs Flutterstone*) Thank you, Mrs Grandway. I'm much obliged to you.

Miss Warburton wanders off, like a lost soul

The rostrum is now in place

Mr Trotter How's that then?

Mrs Grandway That's splendid. Will you get up there, Mrs Flutterstone?

The rostrum is about three feet high. Mrs Flutterstone goes up and looks at it but is unable to get on to it

Mrs Flutterstone How do I get *up* there? I'll need a step, won't I?

Mrs Grandway Have we got a step, Mr Trotter?

Mr Trotter I didn't see one.

Mrs Grandway Can you improvise something?

Mr Trotter I will for tomorrow.

Mrs Grandway Could you manage for tonight somehow, Mrs Flutterstone?

With a long-suffering look at Mrs Grandway, Mrs Flutterstone starts trying to climb up on to the rostrum

No, don't kneel on it! You'll dirty the dress. (*To Mr Trotter*) Help her, would you?

Mr Trotter and Miss Pomerance help her up, not without difficulty

Miss Pomerance Do you have a lot more technicalities to attend to, Mrs Grandway, or are you going to get on with the play?

Mrs Flutterstone There's nothing to sit on.

Mrs Grandway (*getting fed up*) I'm going as fast as I can, Miss Pomerance. (*She refers to her clipboard*) There are still several things to get right yet.

Miss Pomerance I *would* like to *hear* the play before it goes on, you know. You specifically asked me not to come to rehearsals until Dress Rehearsal night and I deferred to your wishes, didn't I? Is it too much to ask that a writer might have just one opportunity to hear the way the lines she has perspired over are going to be delivered, before the public does?

Mrs Grandway You will hear them, Miss Pomerance, I promise you. Any producer will tell you that authors tend to be an inhibiting factor at rehearsals and we're all deeply grateful to you for letting us get on with them without interruption. Now if you will bear with us a little longer, you'll be able to see your brain-child realized to what I hope will be your complete satisfaction.

Mrs Grandway turns her attention to Mr Trotter immediately, leaving Miss Pomerance standing, her mouth open ready to reply

Would you be so kind, Mr Trotter, as to tell Mr Thirlstane to come and let me see him in the Henry the Eighth costume.

Miss Pomerance goes off into the wings, blazing

Mr Trotter Yes, all right, then I'll go and look for a step.

Mr Trotter exits

Mrs Grandway Now, Mrs Flutterstone. If you feel all right up there, I think that will do.

Mrs Flutterstone Have you done with me then? Can I get some warm clothes on?

Mrs Grandway Of *course* I haven't done with you. Mr Trotter has to light you in your new position yet, but he's gone off on another job. Go and get yourself that cup of coffee meanwhile. And if you decide to put a coat over that dress, make sure you don't crease it. I want Britannia to look immaculate. Immaculate.

Mrs Flutterstone lays down her spear and shield in preparation to descend, wondering how she is going to do this without help

Mr Thirlstane enters enveloped in the Henry the Eighth costume which is many sizes too big for him. He is accompanied by Mrs Hamberley and Mrs Pinkerton

Mrs Hamberley They haven't *sent* any padding.

Mrs Pinkerton I did order it. I can show you, I kept a copy of my letter.

Mrs Hamberley I've suggested using cushions but Mrs Pinkerton doesn't think they will work.

Mrs Pinkerton A cushion would just stick out in front. He needs proper body padding. All round.

Mrs Flutterstone How the dickens do I get down off here?

Mrs Hamberley (*haughtily*) I *know* what we *need*—but we haven't *got* proper body padding, have we? We've got to improvise somehow. Please try and be *practical*, Mrs Pinkerton.

Mrs Grandway Do you think we could make some, Mrs Pinkerton?

Mrs Pinkerton Not for tomorrow I couldn't. There are two sets of sleeves to shorten and one to lengthen. And Mrs Burncliffe's Queen Victoria dress is *far* too short.

Mrs Hamberley I *said* the committee shouldn't have cast Mrs Burncliffe as Queen Victoria. She's far too tall!

Mrs Grandway There *was* no-one else.

Mrs Hamberley But Queen Victoria was four feet eleven—or something like that. She was *tiny*!

Mrs Grandway Please don't complicate matters, Mrs Hamberley. It's too late now. And we're trying to deal with Mr Thirlstane. What do you suggest, Mrs Pinkerton?

Mrs Pinkerton I'll try and find some material, if I have time, and put a false bottom on it.

Mrs Hamberley Can't Mrs Burncliffe attend to her own false bottom?

Mrs Pinkerton I asked her if she could but she says she hasn't time. She says it's wardrobe's job.

Mrs Hamberley She can't expect us to do everything!

Mrs Pinkerton Me, you mean. You're the Wardrobe Mistress. That's what it says on the programme! I'm only the Assistant Wardrobe Mistress.

Mrs Flutterstone (*loudly*) How do I get off here, Mrs Grandway?

Mrs Grandway (*deep in thought*) What if Mr Thirlstane wore several jackets underneath, one on top of another. That might do the trick.

Miss Warburton peeps in, then creeps on

Mrs Hamberley I think that's an excellent idea, Mrs Grandway.

Miss Warburton (*in a stage whisper*) Mrs Grandway ...

Mrs Grandway Would you go and try it, Mr Thirlstane?

Miss Warburton (*in a stage whisper*) Mrs Grandway ...

Mr Thirlstane Where do I get the jackets from?

Mrs Grandway Borrow them from the rest of the cast for tonight.

Mr Thirlstane All right. But you can see why Mr Huskisson and myself swopped costumes, can't you? We weren't trying to be awkward. I don't know what you're going to do about *him*, though. He can't get into the Shakespeare costume at all.

Miss Warburton (*persevering*) Mrs Grandway ...

Mrs Flutterstone (*determined*) Could somebody help me off here?

Mrs Grandway Yes, sorry Mrs Flutterstone. Where's Mr Trotter?

Mrs Flutterstone He said he was going to look for a step.

Mrs Pinkerton I don't think it will work.

Mrs Grandway What won't?

Mrs Pinkerton The jackets.

Mrs Grandway Why not?

Mrs Pinkerton Over the sleeves.

Mrs Hamberley You mean it'll look as if he has fat arms?

Miss Warburton (*a little louder*) Mrs Grandway ...

Mrs Pinkerton No, I mean the armholes. It will be too tight under the armholes.

Mrs Grandway Just one moment, Miss Warburton. Do go and see if it works would you, Mrs Pinkerton? We must get this problem sorted out.

Mrs Pinkerton, Mrs Hamberley and Mr Thirlstane go off

Mrs Grandway Now Miss Warburton, what's troubling you?

Miss Warburton It's Mrs Burncliffe. She's crying.

Mrs Grandway Crying?!

Miss Warburton She's sitting in the dressing-room crying her eyes out.

Mrs Grandway What about?

Miss Warburton About her Queen Victoria costume. She says
she's going to look ridiculous in it.

Mrs Grandway Oh, I know about that. Tell her we'll deal with
that shortly. I can't do everything at once.

Miss Warburton She says Queen Victoria never wore a miniskirt,
and *she* won't!

Mrs Grandway But Mrs Pinkerton is going to lengthen it.

Miss Warburton There's nothing to let down.

Mrs Grandway Tell her to stop crying and not be so silly. Mrs
Pinkerton's going to put a false bottom on it.

Miss Warburton Mrs Pinkerton told her she might not have time
to do it.

Mrs Grandway (*with a sigh*) Oh dear! Ask Mrs Burncliffe to come
and let me see it, will you please?

Miss Warburton All right. Thank you. I'm much obliged to you.

*Miss Warburton almost bows herself off, timidly, gratefully,
backwards*

Mrs Grandway Now Mrs Flutterstone—let's see what I can do
about you.

*She tries to help Mrs Flutterstone off the rostrum, but there seems to
be no way. Mrs Flutterstone is bent over and they are holding hands*

Mrs Grandway I don't suppose you could jump. No, perhaps
you'd better not.

Mrs Flutterstone Could you find a chair for me to stand on?

*Mrs Grandway looks around, still holding Mrs Flutterstone's hands,
and sees Miss Pomerance in the wings*

Mrs Grandway (*calling*) Miss Pomerance—would you mind fetching a chair?

Miss Pomerance enters

Miss Pomerance I beg your pardon?

Mrs Grandway I said, would you mind fetching a chair?

Miss Pomerance (*affronted, as if it were beneath her dignity*) A
chair? Me? Where from?

Mrs Grandway Anywhere.

Miss Pomerance Well! I'll see if I can find one.

Miss Pomerance exits

Mrs Grandway What happened to the chair you were sitting on before?

Mrs Flutterstone I've no idea. (*She looks around*) Oh dear, it's here, behind the rostrum.

Mrs Grandway fetches the chair, helps Mrs Flutterstone down, not noticing as:

Miss Warburton enters, still in her Queen Elizabeth dress. She is followed by Mrs Burncliffe, somewhat reluctantly, still crying. Mrs Burncliffe is a tall lady, anxious to please, and most upset because she is causing a fuss. Her Queen Victoria dress comes half-way down her thighs

Mrs Grandway There now, Mrs Flutterstone—go and get your coffee. (*She sees Mrs Burncliffe*) My God!

Mrs Flutterstone If Prince Albert had've seen you like that he'd have *swam* back to wherever he came from.

This makes Mrs Burncliffe cry even more

Mrs Burncliffe (*trying to control her tears*) I don't want to cause difficulties, Mrs Grandway. That's the last thing I want to do. But I can't wear this. Please don't make me wear this.

Miss Pomerance enters carrying a chair. She sees her Queen Victoria, stops dead, drops the chair

Miss Pomerance What on earth's that?

This results in a further howl from Mrs Burncliffe

Mrs Grandway Whoever wore that dress last must have been very short.

Mrs Flutterstone (*going off*) One of the seven dwarfs!

Mrs Flutterstone exits

Miss Warburton They've cut everything away. There's nothing to lengthen it with at all.

Mrs Grandway They're not supposed to do that. Where's Wardrobe?

Miss Warburton Mrs Hamberley and Mrs Pinkerton are attending to Henry the Eighth. Shall I go and fetch them?

Mrs Grandway Would you, please.

Miss Warburton exits

Miss Pomerance Mrs Grandway! I've written a serious play, not a ... a ... *pantomime*! I have a London producer coming down to see the play tomorrow. What's he going to think?! She looks like ... like Widow Twankey!

This produces a further howl from Mrs Burncliffe

You'll have to get a new costume for her.

Mrs Grandway It's too late to get a replacement costume. Let me think!

Miss Pomerance Think? What good is *that* going to do?

Mrs Grandway Do you *mind*, Miss Pomerance! Please don't interfere!

Miss Pomerance sits on the chair she has brought on

Mrs Burncliffe They shouldn't send costumes out like this. It isn't right.

Mrs Grandway (*thinking like mad*) Bend your knees, Mrs Burncliffe, would you?

Mrs Burncliffe Why?

Mrs Grandway I want to see something. Just bend your knees and let the costume drop.

Mrs Burncliffe tries, even getting down on her haunches

Mrs Burncliffe I can't walk about like this!

Mrs Grandway You don't have to walk about in your part. You just have to stand still.

Mrs Burncliffe I won't do it. Don't ask me. I won't do it. Not like this. I know I'm being an awful nuisance but please, Mrs Grandway ...

Mrs Grandway It wouldn't work anyway. I only wanted to try it.

Mrs Burncliffe All my family are coming, too. My sister-in-law is coming over specially—and she lives twenty-five miles away. And she's *very* critical. I'm not going on like this, Mrs Grandway, I'm telling you now. I'm the last person to want to cause any trouble, but I'm not going on like this.

Mrs Hamberley and Mrs Pinkerton enter

Mrs Grandway Ah good! Now what are we going to do about this, Mrs Pinkerton?

Mrs Hamberley (*as if it were her idea*) It needs a long false bottom, doesn't it, Mrs Pinkerton.

Mrs Pinkerton It would look like a sort of large peplum.

Mrs Grandway That would be all right.

Mrs Burncliffe But you said you didn't have time to do it.

Mrs Pinkerton I haven't. I'm going to be up most of the night anyway.

Mrs Flutterstone enters with a large flask and a cup

Mrs Flutterstone Would you like a cup of coffee, Mrs Grandway?

Mrs Grandway No thank you, Mrs Flutterstone, I've got my own.

Mrs Hamberley I wouldn't mind a cup. I didn't have time for any tea.

Mrs Flutterstone I've only enough for two, Mrs Hamberley, and I promised a cup to Florence Nightingale if Mrs Grandway didn't want one.

She goes off, leaving Mrs Hamberley visibly snubbed

Miss Pomerance I agree with Mrs Burncliffe. She can't go on like that!

Mrs Grandway Quite.

Mrs Hamberley What it really needs is a new skirt, over the top. That's what I think.

Mrs Grandway Do you have a black skirt, Mrs Burncliffe? A full-length one?

Mrs Burncliffe I've only got a floral one.

They all shake their heads. Pause

Mrs Pinkerton (*apologetically*) I sent them the measures.

Mrs Grandway (*standing with her back to Miss Pomerance*) I wonder whether Miss Pomerance has a long black skirt. She seems the long black skirt type.

Miss Pomerance (*almost making Mrs Grandway jump*) Do I!? It might interest you to know that I never wear black. Never! Too ... severe. Nor pastel shades. Too docile! I'm a passionate devotee of bright colours.

Mrs Grandway Oh.

Miss Pomerance The plain fact is—it's not the fault of the dress. It's just that Mrs Burncliffe is too tall to play Queen Victoria. Queen Victoria was a very short lady, and the costumiers know

that, even if some producers *don't*. She should never have been
cast in the part.

Mrs Hamberley But she read it beautifully. Didn't you, Mrs
Burncliffe?

Mrs Burncliffe Thank you.

Miss Pomerance Nevertheless. I would have thought you would
have known better, Mrs Grandway.

Mrs Grandway I didn't cast the play, Miss Pomerance. The
Casting Committee did, didn't they Mrs Hamberley? *You*'re on
the Casting Committee.

Mrs Hamberley The Casting Committee were more interested in
the majesty of the part rather than the historical stature of the
character *or* the actress. We wanted Queen Victoria to dominate
in her scene.

Miss Pomerance Yes, well you should have ordered a costume to
match that conception, shouldn't you? She couldn't dominate a
wolf-cubs concert in that!

Mrs Pinkerton I sent them Mrs Burncliffe's measurements. Didn't
I, Mrs Burncliffe. Didn't I measure you?

Mrs Hamberley Could you dye it black?

Mrs Burncliffe What?

Mrs Hamberley Your floral skirt.

Mrs Burncliffe (*affronted*) It's for my husband's Lodge Dinners!

Mrs Pinkerton It mightn't take dye, anyway—not if it's floral.
Floral things don't dye well.

Mrs Hamberley Why do you invariably refute all my suggestions,
Mrs Pinkerton? I'm merely trying to be helpful. I'll go and finish
attending to Mr Thirlstane. *You* can deal with this!

Mrs Hamberley storms off

Mrs Pinkerton She gets offended very easily, doesn't she?

Mr Trotter enters carrying a small two-foot by one-foot rostrum

Mr Trotter I found this, Mrs Grandway. It needs a two-tread
really but it'll be better than nothing. Where's Britannia gone?

Mrs Grandway She's gone for a cup of coffee.

Mr Trotter puts the rostrum down in front of Mrs Burncliffe

Mr Trotter Heavier than it looks, that is. It was down in the cellar.

Mrs Grandway Just a minute! (*A beat*) Stand right behind that rostrum Mrs Burncliffe, will you?

Mrs Burncliffe does so

Closer.

Mrs Burncliffe moves close behind the rostrum, which reaches about up to her knees

That might just do it.
Mr Trotter Do what?
Mrs Grandway If we had *two* like that, Mr Trotter, Mrs Burncliffe could stand behind them.
Miss Pomerance Stand behind them?!
Mrs Grandway We might just get away with it, provided you stood still.
Mrs Burncliffe What about when I come on?
Mrs Grandway I'll have them placed so that they run behind the wing.
Mr Trotter Where am I going to find another like that?
Mrs Grandway Have another look in the cellar. There might be another one.
Mr Trotter There isn't. I'd have seen it.
Mrs Grandway Then you'll have to kneel down behind the one.
Mrs Burncliffe I won't do it, Mrs Grandway. I'll just be a laughing stock. Everybody knows I'm not a little woman. I'm not standing in a hole! I'm not! I won't!
Mrs Grandway (*closing her eyes to command patience*) Mrs Pinkerton is going to try to get your costume lengthened. This is a standby—just in case—a second line of defence.
Mrs Burncliffe (*bursting into tears again*) I knew I should never have taken a part. I'll never live it down, I know I won't.
Mr Trotter Why don't you sit her on a chair, Mrs Grandway. There's a sort of throne in the cellar which we made for Richard the Third a few years ago. Then you could throw a rug over her knees.
Mrs Grandway That's a brilliant idea. I'll bet she often sat with a rug over her knees. Palaces are draughty places, you know.
Mrs Pinkerton I've got a large tartan rug at home.
Mrs Grandway Splendid. Queen Victoria spent a lot of time in Scotland.

Mr Trotter She could have picked one up as a souvenir, couldn't she?

Miss Pomerance I give up!

Miss Pomerance storms off

Mrs Grandway Would you bring the rug tomorrow, Mrs Pinkerton, please.

Mrs Burncliffe (*being escorted off by Mrs Pinkerton*) It won't look right. I know it won't. Heaven knows what my sister-in-law will think . . .

Mrs Burncliffe and Mrs Pinkerton exit

Mr Trotter I'll see if I can find that throne.

Mr Trotter exits. Mrs Hamberley enters from the other side with Mr Thirlstane in the Henry the Eighth costume. He is so much padded that his arms are out at forty-five degrees from his body

Mrs Hamberley How does this look, Mrs Grandway?

Mr Thirlstane I can hardly breathe!

Mrs Grandway I must agree with Mrs Pinkerton, the arms *don't* look right.

Mr Thirlstane (*an appealing look*) *Couldn't* I wear the other costume? It fits me so well.

Mrs Grandway (*ignoring him*) How many jackets has he got on?

Mrs Hamberley Four. We couldn't get any more on over the sleeves.

Mrs Grandway We need some jackets with the sleeves cut out, don't we?

Mrs Hamberley Have you any old suits you don't need, Mr Thirlstane?

Mrs Grandway No. We'll need to buy some that we can cut up. Could you go to a second-hand shop in the morning and buy a few old jackets?

Mrs Hamberley (*haughtily*) I'm not familiar with second-hand shops, Mrs Grandway. I wouldn't know where to find one! Mrs Pinkerton will have to find time to do it.

Mr Thirlstane I'm not wearing second-hand clothes. There won't be time to have them cleaned.

Mrs Grandway They won't be next to your skin, Mr Thirlstane.

Mr Thirlstane And what if it doesn't work? I can't get here tomorrow until about twenty minutes before we go on. There won't even be time to try it out.

Mrs Grandway Twenty minutes? That's cutting it fine, isn't it?

Mr Thirlstane Well I didn't know I'd be working on a job out of town when I took the part, did I?

Mrs Grandway We'll just have to take a chance then. Could you arrange it with Mrs Pinkerton, Mrs Hamberley, please?

Mrs Hamberley I'll try—but I must say, Mrs Pinkerton is getting rather obstreperous. I can't do anything with her today.

Mrs Hamberley exits with Mr Thirlstane, almost crashing into Mr Trotter coming on with the big step-ladder

Mr Trotter Could I just get the Britannia spots refocussed, Mrs Grandway? Albert's ready for me now.

Mrs Grandway All right—but don't be long. Miss Pomerance is——

Mr Trotter I know. Won't be a tick. (*He climbs on to the rostrum and stands in the Britannia position. He calls*) Kill 'em, Albert.

Black-out

Number twenty-seven on its own please, Albert.

A spot comes on, lighting somewhere near the OP wing

Is that number twenty-seven? What's the one on Britannia then? Kill twenty-seven, try twenty-six.

Black-out. Then a red spot comes on elsewhere

That's not it. Are you on the blue panel? Switch on the blue panel master.

The stage goes green

I'll have to come up. Put it back the way it was.

Original lighting returns

Mr Trotter exits with his ladder. Miss Pomerance comes storming on

Miss Pomerance Mrs Grandway—we have to be out of this building by half-past ten. It's now half-past eight. The play takes one and three-quarter hours to perform, even if nothing goes wrong in the middle of it, which it wouldn't surprise me if it did! Do you or do you not think it's time to start the run through!

Mrs Grandway It is *not* half-past eight, Miss Pomerance, it is only half-past seven.

Miss Pomerance My watch says half-past eight! How anyone can presume to direct a historical play when they can't even tell the time is beyond me!

Mrs Grandway (*shielding her eyes from the light to peer at the clock at the back of the hall*) There you are—half-past seven—on the hall clock!

Mr Trotter enters

Mr Trotter (*having heard the foregoing*) That clock's an hour slow, Mrs Grandway. It hasn't been altered since the clocks went forward. Didn't they tell you?

Miss Pomerance (*a victory*) *Thank* you Mr Trotter.

Mrs Grandway And I've been going by it. Very well. That's it! Will you go round, Mr Trotter, and tell everyone that we will begin the Dress Rehearsal in five minutes. Ready or not. Five minutes.

Miss Pomerance (*with a sarcastic but self-satisfied look*) Thank you!

Mr Trotter (*calling out front*) Set your board ready to start, Albert. (*He starts to exit, calling, well into the distance*) Five minutes, everyone. Five minutes ...

Mr Trotter exits. Miss Warburton enters

Miss Warburton She won't go on, Mrs Grandway.

Mrs Grandway Who won't?

Miss Warburton Queen Victoria. Mrs Burncliffe.

Mrs Grandway (*at the end of her tether*) Look—you go and tell Mrs Burncliffe she's *got* to, and not to be so silly!

Miss Warburton She won't. Not in that dress. I know she won't.

But Miss Warburton goes to tell her, nevertheless

A clatter off-stage, followed by a scream

Mrs Grandway What in *heaven's* name is the matter now!

Mrs Pinkerton enters

Mrs Pinkerton (*almost in tears*) It's Britannia! She's just spilled a cup of coffee all down her lovely white dress!

Mrs Flutterstone enters, a great brown stain down her dress and an empty cup in her hand

Mrs Flutterstone You can kill yourself out there! I was just bringing some coffee for Mrs Hamberley ...

Mr Trotter runs on

Mr Trotter What was that? What happened?
Mrs Flutterstone Who the hell left that box, or whatever it is, standing there. Was it you? I tripped right over it. Just look at this mess ...!
Mr Trotter I've got to store the props *somewhere*!
Mrs Flutterstone (*raising her voice*) Well you should look where you're putting it. It's dark there in the wings!
Mr Trotter (*shouting back*) Not if you look where you're going.
Mrs Flutterstone You could maim someone for life!
Mr Trotter A blind man could see it! You've only to look!

Mrs Burncliffe enters followed by Miss Warburton

Mrs Burncliffe I won't do it, Mrs Grandway, you'll have to find someone else.
Mrs Flutterstone (*rubbing her leg*) I've hurt my leg too. There'll be a great black bruise there tomorrow. Good job I'm not wearing *your* costume, Mrs Burncliffe, or everyone would see it.
Mrs Grandway It's too late to get someone else, Mrs Burncliffe. You know very well we go on tomorrow.
Mrs Hamberley Good gracious! What on earth have you done to your dress, Mrs Flutterstone?
Mrs Burncliffe You'll have to go on without me. I'm sorry, but I'm not going to make a fool of myself. I'm not. Not in front of my sister-in-law.
Mrs Flutterstone What am I going to do with this dress then?
Mrs Hamberley You'll have to wash it tonight and hope it comes out.
Mrs Flutterstone Hey, listen! *You*'re the Wardrobe Mistress. *You* wash it.
Mrs Hamberley I'm not washing your clothes after *you*. You spilled the coffee down it, you wash it.

Mrs Flutterstone I was bringing the damned coffee for *you*.

Mrs Burncliffe I won't do it. I won't go on.

Mrs Hamberley Doesn't matter where you were taking the coffee. Doesn't make it *my* fault!

Mrs Flutterstone (*pointing at Mr Trotter*) It was *his* fault. *He* should get it washed.

Mrs Pinkerton I'll wash it—but I'm not sure if coffee stains will come out of white completely.

Mrs Grandway Thank you, Mrs Pinkerton. If they don't she'll have to wear a white apron over the top.

Mrs Flutterstone Look—I'm playing Britannia, not a waitress at the *Black Bull!*

Miss Pomerance Are you going to start the play or aren't you. If not, I'm going home.

Mr Thirlstane enters in the Shakespeare costume again, but wearing a crown and carrying an orb and sceptre

Mr Thirlstane Mr Huskisson says this won't look too bad for Henry the Eighth, with the crown on and these things. Every-one'll know I'm the King.

Mrs Grandway But if you wear that what's Shakespeare going to wear?

Mr Thirlstane Mr Huskisson's putting the Henry the Eighth costume on now for you to see. They'll have to imagine that Shakespeare's got his best suit on, that's all. Perhaps Miss Pomerance could put a line in to that effect.

Miss Pomerance Miss Pomerance will do no such thing!

Mr Thirlstane Why not? They won't know.

Mrs Hamberley The headmaster of St Bartholomew's will!

Mrs Burncliffe I won't go on. Not in this.

Miss Pomerance Mrs Grandway . . .!!

Mrs Grandway All right, I know what you're going to say, so please don't say it! (*Firmly*) Now listen everybody! That's enough! We'll get the problems sorted out tomorrow, I promise you. We're going to start. In four minutes. Go and get ready. Go on!

Reluctantly, they all troop off, except Miss Pomerance

Miss Pomerance It's going to be a disaster, isn't it? I know it is. I should never have promised to——

Mrs Grandway No it isn't! They're worried because they want the show to be good. They want everything to be right, just as I do, because they're keen, and dedicated. They've given up their evenings to come to rehearsals and stayed up half the night learning their lines, and practising the best way to deliver them. It isn't Mrs Burncliffe's fault that her costume isn't right yet, isn't what she'd imagined it would be, nor is it my fault—or yours. She's more worried that she'll look wrong in the play than what her sister-in-law thinks, believe me. If the play fails it won't be their fault. They've all done their very best. Perhaps I should have asked you to stay away until tomorrow night. There are always problems at Dress Rehearsals, particularly with a costume show. This is your first stage play, or you'd know that. We'll get everything ironed out before seven-thirty tomorrow, you'll see.

Mr Trotter comes back on

Mr Trotter Can we set the first scene, Mrs Grandway?
Mrs Grandway Yes of course.
Mr Trotter (*calling to the wing*) Drop the curtain, Fred.

The curtain falls behind him

(*He calls to the back*) House lights, Albert.

As he disappears through the curtain the house Lights come on

FURNITURE AND PROPERTY LIST

On stage: Union Jack
Chair

Off stage: Step-ladder **(Mr Trotter)**
2 rostra **(Mr Trotter)**
Chair **(Miss Pomerance)**
Flask and cup **(Mrs Flutterstone)**
Padding **(Mr Thirlstane)**
Brown stain **(Mrs Flutterstone)**
Crown, orb and sceptre **(Mr Thirlstane)**

Personal: Shield and spear **(Mrs Flutterstone)**
Clipboard **(Mrs Grandway)**
Watch **(Miss Pomerance)**

LIGHTING PLOT

Property fittings required: nil

To open: Full general lighting

Cue 1	**Mr Trotter:** "Check the fuse." *Black-out*	(Page 4)
Cue 2	**Mr Trotter:** "Not the main fuse, you nit!" *Bring up general lighting*	(Page 4)
Cue 3	**Mr Trotter:** "Kill 'em, Albert." *Black-out*	(Page 20)
Cue 4	**Mr Trotter:** "Number twenty-seven on its own ..." *Switch on spot to cover* R *wing*	(Page 20)
Cue 5	**Mr Trotter:** "Kill twenty-seven, try twenty-six." *Black-out. Then snap on red spot*	(Page 20)
Cue 6	**Mr Trotter:** "Switch on the blue panel master." *Bring up green Lights*	(Page 20)
Cue 7	**Mr Trotter:** "Put it back the way it was." *Revert to general lighting*	(Page 20)
Cue 8	**Mr Trotter:** "House lights, Albert." *Bring up a house Lights*	(Page 24)

EFFECTS PLOT

Cue 1   **Miss Warburton** exits   (Page 21)
            Clatter off-stage, followed by a scream